BEYOND THE LEMONADE STAND

Starting Small to Make It BIG!

By Bill Rancic
winner of THE APPRENTICE

With Karen Soenen

razOr
bill

For our mom—who taught us the importance of family, how to enjoy life, love others, appreciate what we have, and of course . . . make lemonade.

Beyond the Lemonade Stand: Starting Small to Make It BIG!

RAZORBILL

Published by the Penguin Group
Penguin Young Readers Group
345 Hudson Street, New York, New York 10014, U.S.A.
Penguin Group (USA) Inc., 375 Hudson Street, New York, New York 10014, U.S.A.
Penguin Group (Canada), 90 Eglinton Avenue, Suite 700, Toronto, Ontario, Canada M4P 2Y3
(a division of Pearson Penguin Canada Inc.)
Penguin Books Ltd, 80 Strand, London WC2R 0RL, England
Penguin Ireland, 25 St Stephen's Green, Dublin 2, Ireland (a division of Penguin Books Ltd)
Penguin Group (Australia), 250 Camberwell Road, Camberwell, Victoria 3124, Australia
(a division of Pearson Australia Group Pty Ltd)
Penguin Books India Pvt Ltd, 11 Community Centre, Panchsheel Park,
New Delhi – 110 017, India
Penguin Group (NZ), Cnr Airborne and Rosedale Roads, Albany, Auckland 1310,
New Zealand (a division of Pearson New Zealand Ltd)
Penguin Books (South Africa) (Pty) Ltd, 24 Sturdee Avenue, Rosebank, Johannesburg 2196,
South Africa

Penguin Books Ltd, Registered Offices: 80 Strand, London WC2R 0RL, England

10 9 8 7 6 5 4 3 2 1

Library of Congress Cataloging-in-Publication Data is available

Printed in the United States of America

WHAT'S INSIDE

Dear Reader,

Welcome to *Beyond the Lemonade Stand: Starting Small to Make It BIG!* It's kind of a long title, but there are a couple of important reasons that I chose it.

First, my *very first job* was running a lemonade stand at the end of my driveway with my big sisters. I was eight years old when I ran that stand. Talk about "starting small"!

I learned a lot from that job (including how to get along with my sisters), and it taught me lessons I still use today.

Second, when I landed a spot on the first season of *The Apprentice*, I couldn't have been happier. I thought I had made it big! Then came the moment we had all been waiting for—Donald Trump gathered us together to tell us about our first task. I wondered, *What can it be? Putting together a big deal for one of Mr. Trump's properties? Trading stocks on the New York Stock Exchange?*

Nope. It was *selling lemonade!*

Which goes to show something we already know: every business venture—no matter how small—is worthwhile. And every entrepreneur, no matter how young, can become a big success! (An *entrepreneur* is anyone who starts his or her own business.)

You can become one too.

Chances are, if you're reading this introduction, you're a lot like I was as a kid. You're focused, you're smart, and you want to show the world that you're ready to succeed! I wrote this book to help you do just that.

In the grown-up world, when we start a new business, we call it a *venture*. But I prefer to think of each new business as an *adventure*—a chance to learn something about yourself and the people around you while, hopefully, making some cash.

In the following chapters, you'll learn a lot about some of my very first business adventures. Whether they were successful or not (and many were not), I definitely gained something valuable from each experience. So, after each story, I'll tell you about some of the lessons I learned and maybe give you and your friends something to talk about.

You'll also find out how some really important people got their starts—as kid entrepreneurs just like you. They'll share their secrets for success and give you a head start.

After that, you'll find some business ideas that you may want to try—either on your own or with a friend. There are some simple ideas that are a snap to set up—but there are also ideas that go *beyond the lemonade stand* to tap into the things *you* like to do—the things *you're* good at!

Finally, and most importantly, we'll talk about what truly matters in business—and what success really means.

Many people think that the definition of success is making as much money as you can in the shortest amount of time possible. I disagree; in fact, I've seen many people go down that road—only to find a dead end.

Business should be fun and filled with new and exciting challenges every day. If you focus on four simple rules, like I did, you'll be happy as a kid entrepreneur—whether you strike it rich right away or make a few mistakes on the road to success:

1. Have passion and truly enjoy what you do.

2. Make sure you're honest with people and always honor your word; your honor is the most valuable business asset you have.

3. Work hard—if you try your best, that's the best you can do. Work your hardest and you will never, ever have any regrets, even if you don't do as well as you hoped.

4. Look for ways to "give back." Anytime you can, lend a helping hand to people who need it.

Helping others will make you feel better than all the money in the world. I know, because I volunteer for a ton of worthwhile causes. Even the royalties from this book will go to help kids who need it!

When I was growing up, my parents always taught me that it was okay to try different things. Some of my business ventures were bound to be winners—and some were bound to be losers.

My parents reminded me that even if I lost, every experience would be a learning experience. I'd gain some valuable knowledge if I just paid attention.

Well, I guess I paid attention, because I *did* learn some important things along the way. Now I'm excited to share them with you!

So let's get started! It's time to make it big!

Bill

PART 1

Ideas and Inspiration

Take a look through these thoughts
from me and some of my friends
before you start on your own business
adventure.

MAKE LEMONADE!

Who doesn't like lemonade?

Who hasn't set up a lemonade stand?

How difficult could it be?

Those were the thoughts racing through my ten-year-old brain on a sweltering hot morning in late August.

Why was I thinking about lemonade? Because I *needed* the new skateboard my friends had, and there was only one way I was going to get it.

Christmas was four months away, and my birthday had just passed. No one was going to give me the skateboard anytime soon, so I had to take action. I had to earn the money and buy the skateboard myself. A lemonade stand, I thought, was the perfect solution.

I talked my buddies Luke and Jake into helping me out. Then I borrowed a few dollars from my mom, and in the sweetest voice I could muster asked if she would "please, please, please" take me to the grocery store to buy lemonade and paper cups. She said yes, and before long, I was in business.

Or so I thought. After mixing up the lemonade in a big pitcher, the three of us set up shop in a key location, which happened to be the end of my driveway. We priced the lemonade at fifty cents a cup and waited.

"Here comes a car!" I yelled. "We have a customer!" I stood up straight, prepared to make my first sale, but no sooner were those words out of my mouth than I found myself staring at the taillights of that car. It zoomed right by us without anyone purchasing even one crummy cup of lemonade!

During the next hour, I counted only five cars that went by my driveway, and out of those cars, only one of them stopped to make a purchase. I had spent four dollars on supplies and after one and a half hours only made a buck back!

My new skateboard was getting further and further out of sight by the minute.

I knew something was wrong with my plan. I had to change things around. That was when it struck me, a brilliant idea. I asked Luke if we could borrow his little brother's wagon.

We packed up cups and ice and took our show—or in this case lemonade—on the road. I was going door-to-door! Within the next hour we had covered half the neighborhood and sold twenty cups of lemonade.

It was the hardest day of work I had ever put in, but by

nightfall, I had enough money to buy that skateboard I so desperately wanted.

LESSON LEARNED: In business, you need to be adaptable and change your game plan if the one you have isn't working.

THINK ABOUT THIS: What should you do when you have an idea that doesn't seem to be working? Think about a difficult time you had lately and how it might have gone differently with some quick, creative thinking.

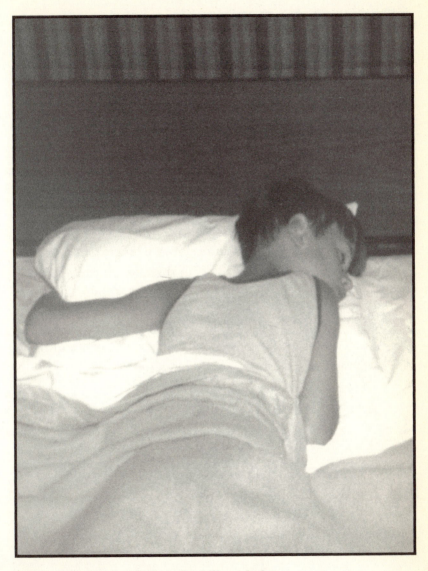

After a hard day's work, I slept like a baby.

THINGS TO THINK ABOUT . . .

Learn how to market yourself

Think hard. . . . What are you really good at? What makes you *you*? Are you a fast learner? Are you organized? Are you strong? Are you a hard worker?

Recognize your strengths and let people know about them. When you can play up your strengths, others can see your talents more easily.

Also, think about specific things that you enjoy and find a way to make them a part of your business. If you're extremely talented in computers, find a business in that area. If you're good at art, create a portfolio that includes samples of your work that everyone can see.

When you're doing something that you're talented in, you can go far and enjoy yourself at the same time!

KID'S CORNER

Kids like you talk about their own business (ad)ventures.

Gerry Stank, age 7

Last summer, I collected the cans and bottles from my house that had a deposit on them and turned them in at the grocery store. It wasn't hard and I made money.

Also, there was a construction crew working down the street. I loaded some lemonade into a wagon and pulled it down the street. All the construction workers bought lemonade and I made a lot of money.

LESSON LEARNED: Just look around for ways to make money.

PANCAKES AND PROFIT!

It was a summer day in late June when my mom and dad decided to take everyone in the family on vacation. Everyone, that is, except for me. You see, I'm the youngest in my family and the only boy. This vacation was going to be especially for my sisters, and my parents figured that I would have more fun staying with my grandma for the weekend. Now, I loved Grandma, that's for sure. But a whole weekend together? Just her and me? I was skeptical about it, but I didn't have much of a choice.

So, on Friday afternoon, with a suitcase in my hand, I got into the backseat of my dad's car. Little did I know, I wasn't just going to visit my grandmother, I was about to start my very first business!

The first day at Grandma Rancic's house, Grandma and I did the usual stuff. She paraded me around to all of her neighbor friends so they could pinch my cheeks and tell me how big I had gotten. Then we went to visit Uncle Joe "A.T.A." (The *a.t.a.* got tagged onto his name because he lived "across the alley" from Grandma Rancic.) Uncle Joe and I walked to the grocery store to stock up for the weekend. Grandma always made sure she had my favorite foods in the house, and one of those was pancakes.

The next morning was Saturday, and as always, I woke up very early in the morning. By 9:00 a.m. I was so bored I couldn't imagine what I would do to pass the time till my parents came home. That was when I decided to help my grandmother make breakfast.

Grandma showed me how to make my favorite pancakes. We stirred the batter, poured it, and cooked the pancakes to golden perfection. My very first batch came out so well that I couldn't help feeling proud. In fact, I was so proud that I wanted to share my newfound talent—with none other than the cheek-pinching neighbor ladies! I had Grandma invite them over, and I placed three perfectly round, delicious pancakes in front of each one of them.

Grandma's friends raved and raved about my pancakes. How light and fluffy they were, how even the ones at the restaurant up the street couldn't compare. Things were starting to look up! I liked cooking for people. Maybe Grandma could teach me some more—and this weekend wouldn't be so boring after all.

After breakfast, I started to clean up. I lifted a plate to bring it to the sink and gasped in surprise. There was a five-dollar bill under the plate! In fact, there was a crisp five-dollar bill under *every* plate. It was like I had won the lottery!

As I got ready for bed that night, I started thinking about what I would do with the fifteen dollars I had earned that day. And I started wondering how I could get even more money. Hey, if I saved enough of it, maybe I could open my own pancake restaurant someday.

On Sunday night, when my mom and dad came to pick me up, they gave me souvenirs from their trip, but nothing could compare with the money I had made on Saturday morning.

When Monday came, I had only one thing on my mind— asking if I could go to my grandmother's house again next weekend. After all, those ladies were hungry for my pancakes, and I was making a tasty profit!

LESSON LEARNED: Recognize an opportunity. It may come in the most unexpected ways from the most unexpected places.

THINK ABOUT THIS: What do you most enjoy doing? What are your talents? Is there any way to create a business opportunity around those talents?

Grandma Rancic and me at her house, where I learned to make pancakes.

WORDS OF WISDOM

Today's most successful people were once kids just like you. Check out their words of wisdom, and learn the secret to their success.

Whether you're a kid starting your first business, or an adult still chasing success, the most important thing to remember is to never give up—never, ever give up!

If you have a dream that you believe in with your whole heart, you have to go after it. Even when others are telling you that you can't do it.

If you give something your best effort, your very best effort, there is a very good chance that you will succeed. And even if you don't, you will be able to say you gave it your all. That's what makes you a winner.

—Donald J. Trump
Billionaire real estate developer

KID'S CORNER

Kids like you talk about their own business (ad)ventures.

Katie Reynaldo, age 12

My family had a garage sale. My sisters and I sold all the things we didn't want anymore. I made a lot of money with the things I sold. My mom told us that we could to keep some of the money and give some of it to charity to help the poor families in our neighborhood. It felt good to have the money, but it felt better to help someone who needed it.

LESSON LEARNED: When you have money, it feels good to give some of it to people who don't have as much as you.

ADVENTURES IN BABYSITTING

I had a lot of babysitters in my day.

I can vividly remember Jean, or, as we called her, Mean Jean. She never played with us and always insisted that we go to bed on time. My sisters and I begged our parents to come home early on the nights Jean was babysitting.

Then there was Susan, who we couldn't wait to have over. She always brought along a huge cardboard box filled with toys and games to keep us occupied.

So by the time my twelfth birthday came along, I was a babysitting expert. I had seen the best and the worst of them. More importantly, I had seen my older sisters make money babysitting neighborhood kids. I decided to do them one better. I was going to start a mini day-care business in my basement!

I decided to handle three kids at a time, max. The kids would come over to my house and hang out in their own super-cool playroom, filled with toys. They'd have so much fun they'd tell their friends, and business would boom.

The first thing I did was get the playroom in the basement ready. Growing up with three sisters, the dolls and tea sets were plentiful. Even though I claimed they always had more "stuff" than I did, I had my fair share of cars and trucks to play with too. I prepared healthy snacks and did my own version of "child-proofing," making sure the area was safe for little kids.

Next, I began advertising my day-care services. I made up my own flyers and hand-delivered them door-to-door. I started out with one family, and within a week word about my business spread. I had more kids than I could handle at one time!

One day, I was overbooked. I had four children coming over, and I needed backup! My friend Kyle needed to make a few bucks, so I asked him to help out.

I agreed to pay Kyle half of my fee, which meant he would get fifteen dollars. Kyle agreed, and we were all set to go. Then I got a call. Two of the kids I was supposed to babysit were sick.

No sooner had I hung up the phone than Kyle showed up at the door, all ready to work. I had agreed to pay him, but now Kyle would get *all* the money!

I could have sent Kyle home, but I knew I had to keep my word to him. It was my business, and I had to take responsibility. I couldn't back out on my friend. So, I gave Kyle his share, we played with the two kids, and I knew our friendship was worth more than any amount of money could buy.

LESSON LEARNED: Be loyal to your friends and honor your word.

THINK ABOUT THIS: Was there ever a time when you put a material item before your friendships and regretted it later?

I still have a knack for taking care of kids. Here's a picture of me with my nephew Luke.

KID'S CORNER

Kids like you talk about their own business (ad)ventures.

Megan Byerly, age 10

One time in the summer my cousin Zach and I were very bored, so we asked my aunt Tammi if we could set up a lemonade and popcorn stand. We thought that if the customers ate popcorn, they would get thirsty and buy lemonade. My cousin and I fought about who should get the most money. He said, "It's my house, so I should get the most money." But I said, "We both did the stand, so it should be equal." It went back and forth, but my aunt settled it.

LESSON LEARNED: Decide how you're going to divide your earnings before you open your business.

THINGS TO THINK ABOUT . . .

Don't be afraid to ask the experts for advice

Did you ever have a problem understanding something in school? Who did you ask for help? The teacher, of course. The expert!

We all learn from others, and I decided early on not to be too proud to ask others for advice. After all, no one knows *everything*. If you're stuck on a particular problem and know somebody who has been successful, ask about their experiences and listen to what they have to say.

Currently, I'm working with Donald Trump. I ask for his opinion pretty frequently. I'm always able to learn something new from what he has to say.

Just remember, in business, no matter how much advice you get from others, in the end *you* must decide whether that advice is right for you and whether you'll follow it.

KID'S CORNER

Kids like you talk about their own business (ad)ventures.

Shay Decker, age 10

When I was younger, my mom would come home from the store with *lots* of fruit. I would take all the fruit, bring it to the table outside by the end of the driveway, and start a fruit sale. I had a sign out on the table that said FRUIT 25¢ and had some pictures of fruit. Now and then people would drive by and buy an apple or an orange. I would stay outside until it started to get dark. Then I packed up everything and took it inside, and if there was any fruit left over, I would give it to my mom. My mom would be mad because the fruit was like a dollar apiece and I was selling it for twenty-five cents and she was getting ripped off.

LESSON LEARNED: Figure out how much things cost before you decide the price of your product.

KID'S CORNER

Kids like you talk about their own business (ad)ventures.

Yuvraj Duggal, age 10

One day my dad and I wanted to start a neighborhood business. After days of arguing with him about what we were going to do, we decided to start a car wash. We took a two-foot-tall white dry-erase board and put it on the bright green grass. On the board my dad wrote in big letters: TWO-DOOR CARS, $2.00; FOUR-DOOR CARS, $4.00. Before we knew it, we were making a lot of moola. My dad would squirt liquid soap on the car and scrub it, then the driver would pull up some more and I would spray the car with water. Soon my dad went inside and my good friend Aaron came by and took over. When it got dark out and we closed up, we had made three hundred dollars. I divided it into three and gave my friend and my dad a hundred dollars each.

LESSON LEARNED: A big, eye-catching sign is a great way to attract business.

MY FIRST PAPER ROUTE

By the time I was ten years old, I had done odd jobs for my parents and my grandma and even worked for some of the neighbors.

When my next birthday rolled around, I decided things were going to be different. I was going to have a *real* job. I was going to get my very own paper route.

I dialed the number on the bottom of the penny-saver newspaper and told the voice on the other end that I wanted to apply for the newspaper delivery position. The woman on the other end asked how old I was. I told her, and she said she was willing to give me a try.

I thanked her and had barely hung up the phone when a gigantic stack of newspapers was dropped off on my front porch! It looked like Mount Everest! There was also an enormous box of rubber bands and a bag to hold all of the papers across my shoulder.

I didn't have to sign a contract, but my parents made me agree to a six-month commitment to the job. At the time, I wanted the paper route so badly that six months seemed like nothing. I was planning on delivering papers till I could retire rich!

I rolled up my sleeves and started folding the mountain of newspapers in front of me. What seemed like a decade later, all of the papers were neatly rolled and stacked in my bag. Now it was time to begin the route. It wouldn't be a difficult route for me to remember because it consisted of *every house* in the neighborhood. Yep, all one hundred of them. You see, the penny saver was *free* and got delivered to everyone—whether they wanted it or not.

With the bag over my shoulder, I started on my route. It was much more time consuming than I thought it would be—and scarier! I had to deliver to a creepy house on Newgate Court (I left that paper at the *end* of that driveway) and almost had my arm chewed off by the Millers' dog!

Then something even worse happened. I had to walk by the park, where I spotted all of my friends laughing, joking around, and playing my favorite game in the world, the game summers are made for—baseball. That did it. I was going to quit right then and there. I wanted a paycheck, not all of this work and no fun.

As I walked up to the guys on the field, I passed a Dumpster. A tempting thought ran through my mind. *Why don't I just "accidentally" throw the remaining papers into the garbage can? Who would know?* No one was actually paying for the paper, so it wasn't like anyone would miss it.

Then my conscience got the better of me. I remembered the confidence my boss from the penny saver had in me. I also remembered my six-month contract. I told the guys I would be back later and continued on my way.

For the next six months I continued delivering my papers. There were plenty of nice days when my friends were at the park playing sports—and many cold Chicago winter days when outside was the last place I wanted to be—but I kept plugging away at my paper route, making sure every house got its penny saver.

Then one day I got a call from my boss. When I hung up, I was smiling ear to ear. My mom asked what happened. I told her that my boss had put a survey in last week's paper. I received so many compliments from the people on my route that my boss gave me a twenty-five-dollar bonus!

LESSON LEARNED: In the long run, commitment and hard work pay off.

THINK ABOUT THIS: Was there ever a time when you were tempted to quit something you had committed to? What made you change your mind? Think about the rewards of sticking with your commitments before you throw in the towel.

Even though delivering papers was hard work, I enjoyed doing a good job—and I still had time to play.

KID'S CORNER

Kids like you talk about their own business (ad)ventures.

Patrick Hardy, age 10

One time my grandma asked me if I could do her a favor by tearing all the wallpaper off the walls of her downstairs hallway and bathroom. I would be paid for doing this favor.

I had done this kind of work before, when I'd torn all the wallpaper off the walls in my room so I could re-paint it. My room had been easy. All the wallpaper had peeled off in one big sheet. My grandma's wasn't so easy. What I thought would be a couple-hour job turned into days, which eventually turned into weeks of tedious work.

I worked every day, picking tiny pieces of paper off the walls. It was frustrating, but I had made a commitment to my grandma, and I knew I had to follow through with it.

LESSON LEARNED: Even if a job ends up being a hundred times harder than you expected, you shouldn't just quit.

THINGS TO THINK ABOUT . . .

Don't be afraid to be first

Everybody remembers that Neil Armstrong was the first man to walk on the moon, but few people remember who was second. If you're the first person you know of to come up with a great idea, don't be afraid to try it.

Don't be afraid to take a risk.

It's always better to be a leader than a follower.

KID'S CORNER

Kids like you talk about their own business (ad)ventures.

Kyle Stone, age 10

I sold comics. They were mostly about superheroes and vegetables.

One of my vegetables was named Large Lumpy Lettuce. One of my superheroes' names was Reflex Boy. He could run super-fast and make tornadoes.

Me and my three friends, Eric, Elliott, and Kevin, sold our comics for ten cents each.

LESSON LEARNED: You always have to split the money you made with your partners. Most of all, have fun!

PILING UP

At school, every now and again my class would participate in community events. These came in many different forms—from a couple of hours of work here and there to weekend projects. One day, we were asked to rake up leaves at the park.

I wasn't thrilled. There were hundreds and hundreds of old, huge trees in the park. Can you imagine the amount of leaves they dropped every fall?

Unfortunately, I didn't have much of a choice.

I signed up for the first Saturday in October, which turned out to be a beautiful day in Chicago. I headed to the park about noon and set out to complete the job. I raked and raked and raked till I had four humongous piles of leaves. That was when I realized that I had forgotten the bags that I had to put all of the leaves in! I walked home to get the bags, and when I arrived, my parents thought I was finished with my job. They announced that they were taking the family out for pizza and a movie.

I can bag the leaves tomorrow, I thought as I changed my clothes for dinner.

My family and I had a fabulous time. We even got to go to the make-your-own-ice-cream-sundae bar they had at the restaurant.

The next day was Sunday, and I remembered I had to finish my leaf project. I collected some bags and headed over to the park to bag up my piles.

"Oh no!" I said as I walked closer to where my mountains of leaves had been. All the piles were gone!

That was because the night before, while I was out enjoying pizza, the winds had picked up and blown the leaves back to their original place—all over the grass.

So there I was, back to square one. If I had only taken the extra half hour the night before, I would have been saved from repeating the two-hour job that lay ahead of me.

LESSON LEARNED: Don't procrastinate.

THINK ABOUT THIS: Did you ever put off doing something like homework and wish you'd done it right away? Can you find ways to save time by not putting things off till the last minute?

Mom was the one who always told me, "Don't put off till tomorrow what you can do today!"

KID'S CORNER

Kids like you talk about their own business (ad)ventures.

Krstina Harvel, age 9

I plan to become a very good artist and sell my pictures everywhere I go. I have a painting easel at home. My sister and I have a little art studio with markers and crayons. But before I can do that, I need to practice drawing—a lot.

LESSON LEARNED: Practice a lot before going into business.

WORDS OF WISDOM

Today's most successful people were once kids just like you. Check out their words of wisdom, and learn the secret to their success.

Growing up with a brother who had a successful tennis career, knowing that I wanted to follow in his footsteps, I chose every opportunity to watch and learn from his successes and failures. At one of his tournaments, at age eleven, I noticed a major sponsor who had just recently signed him to their company was watching one of his matches. I chose this opportunity to go up this person and introduce myself and tell them about my budding career. I ended up making a big impression on this person, and it was the start of a ten-year business relationship.

LESSON LEARNED: It's never too early to start making contacts in the business world. Networking is one of the most important business skills to master, so be sure to take every opportunity to do so, as you never know what may come of it.

—Andy Roddick
Tennis champion

KID'S CORNER

Kids like you talk about their own business (ad)ventures.

Sloane Decker, age 10

When I was little, I had a bracelet-making kit and I would make bracelets for fifty cents. It was extremely fun, especially when my friends helped me. I would get really excited when people bought a bracelet and let me keep the change. I ended up earning $12.50. I was very proud of myself.

LESSON LEARNED: Sometimes the best way to make money is by doing something you enjoy.

THINGS TO THINK ABOUT . . .

Treat your customers well

Do you know what that means? It means that you should always do what you say, say what you do, and do a little more than is expected.

It means being on time and staying until the job is done. It means being honest, trustworthy, and reliable.

When you treat your customers well, they will certainly hire you again for the same job *and* tell their friends and neighbors what a good worker you are.

That's nice, of course. But the best reward for treating your customers well is hearing someone say, "Thank you. Good job!"

KID'S CORNER

Kids like you talk about their own business (ad)ventures.

Chris Youssef, age 10

One day we wanted to start a dog wash because there were a lot of dogs in our neighborhood. We went to the store and bought the supplies. It took us about seven weeks to build and get our first customer. He said that his dog was so dirty he would give us triple our fee. He told everybody and in a few minutes we had a long, long, long line. That day we made over $150.

LESSON LEARNED: Word of mouth can be a great way to advertise.

TURF TROUBLE!

When I was younger, my dad showed me the finer points of lawn mowing. After spending a week as an "apprentice" to him, he decided to pay me to mow the lawn myself—all summer long.

I don't know who was happier, my dad because he didn't have to mow anymore or me because I could earn ten dollars a week!

Our neighbors saw me hard at work as they drove by, and they noticed that I took care in what I was doing, making sure not to miss any spots. Pretty soon, they asked me to mow their lawns when they went on vacation. I stood up proud and gladly accepted the jobs.

One summer the Grunt family was taking their annual trip to Lake Geneva, Wisconsin. Mr. Grunt asked me to take care of his lawn while he was away. He showed me where his mower was, what trees needed watering, and where the sprinklers were. The following Tuesday, I was set to go. I put on my Walkman (today I guess it would be my MP3 player) and went to work.

Wow, this is easy, I thought. You see, my dad's lawn mower was the old-fashioned kind—the type I had to push. This lawn mower was gasoline powered. It went by itself.

I breezed through the front yard, took a water break, and headed for the back. I was about halfway through the lawn there when I heard what sounded like a crash of lightning, and the mower came to a dead stop.

I looked behind me and found the large twig I'd run over—with something shiny next to it. I bent over to take a look. That shiny object was the lawn mower blade. It had broken off!

I put the Grunts' mower in their garage, got out my dad's mower, and finished the job. But there was still a problem. The Grunt family would be home in three days.

I wish I could say I did the right thing, but I didn't. I ignored the problem, thinking it would go away. It didn't. On the day the Grunts came home, I had a stomachache all day. When the doorbell rang, my heart sank. It was Mr. Grunt. I thought for sure I was in trouble.

Mr. Grunt commented on how nice the lawn looked and gave me ten dollars. This was it! My chance to tell him what happened! But I couldn't muster up the courage. I said good-bye and felt even sicker to my stomach.

The next day, while I was outside playing, I saw Mr. Grunt come out of his garage pushing his mower. He couldn't get it working and began walking my way. Mr. Grunt asked me if I knew anything about what had happened to his lawn mower.

Finally, I told him about the broken blade. Mr. Grunt just shook his head and said he had been to the hardware store earlier that day. If he had known about the lawn mower, he could have picked up a new blade.

I felt awful, and I wanted to make up for my mistake. I offered Mr. Grunt some free mowing, but I knew it would have been easier for me to tell the truth from the beginning. It would have saved me a bunch of stomachaches—and Mr. Grunt another trip to the store.

LESSON LEARNED: In business, take responsibility for your mistakes. Tell the truth. Be honest, even when it's hard to do.

THINK ABOUT THIS: Was there ever a time when a lie seemed easier than the truth to you? What would have happened if you had taken the high road instead of fibbing?

Me with my dad. Not only did he show me how to mow lawns, he told me to always be honest. (Check out my hair in this picture. I don't recommend starting your own haircutting business unless you are specially trained.)

KID'S CORNER

Kids like you talk about their own business (ad)ventures.

Jorie Pristo, age 10

One day I was bored, so my mom took me to the mall. We went into this really expensive store. They had all sorts of cards there that were six dollars apiece. I suddenly had a lightbulb over my head. I thought, *Why don't I start a card business?* I told my mom to rush us home, and once we got there, I brought out glue, glitter, and scissors and started writing and drawing. It took a long time, but I finally finished eight pretty cool cards!

LESSON LEARNED: Believe in what you're doing, and never give up until you are successful!

KID'S CORNER

Kids like you talk about their own business (ad)ventures.

Grace Kelly, age 10

Just a few months ago I learned that my friend was diagnosed with diabetes. His brothers were upset about this because they didn't know if it would keep him from doing things that they liked to do together. They wanted everyone to know what they thought about diabetes. To let them know, they needed a really good idea.

Then they saw everyone was wearing wristbands that said something important, so they decided to make bands that said something too. So they found a company that would make them. They made bands that said SHAME ON SUGAR. They ended up using the money they made from the bracelets for their brother's needs.

LESSON LEARNED: Being a big success isn't always about loading up your piggy bank. Sometimes you can be a big success by helping others.

LET IT SNOW

Winters in Chicago can be very, very long.

One January day I was outside playing in the snow when my dad asked me to help him shovel the driveway. I helped out, and when my friends Jerry and Adam came over, they joined in too. We were finished so quickly that I decided to take my shovel and see if any of the neighbors were interested in having their driveways shoveled too.

My third stop was the home of Mr. Stowe. I rang the doorbell, and when he answered, I noticed he was wearing a bathrobe. He didn't look like his normal energetic self. I offered up my services and he said he would like to hire me not only for that day but for the rest of the winter. "I'm having surgery on my back next week, and I can use all the help I can get," he said. Mr. Stowe was a widower and lived all alone. I gladly accepted the job and was thrilled to have a steady income for the rest of the winter.

Two weeks passed and we got another big snowfall. I bundled up to go outside and shovel Mr. Stowe's driveway. It was so cold out that day, all you could see were my eyes peering out from above my scarf!

With a shovel in hand I headed over to Mr. Stowe's house. As I began my work, I noticed an unusual amount of activity going on at his house. Neighbors were stopping by, leaving off pies, soups, and casseroles. Mr. Stowe answered the door and graciously accepted the offerings of all the neighbors. I finished up the driveway and sauntered up to the door to collect my money. Mr. Stowe was so appreciative that I was able to help him out. He gave me ten dollars plus a two-dollar tip and I was on my way home.

I had only traveled about half a block when I noticed something. I wasn't as happy as I normally was with a fresh ten-dollar bill in my pocket. Mr. Stowe didn't look well. Here the neighbors were dropping off food, sending him get-well cards. . . . I just didn't feel right. I did an about-face and marched right back up to the door. I didn't want to bother Mr. Stowe, so I carefully took the money out of my pocket and slipped it back under his door.

As I walked away from his house, I realized I felt different. My head was held high. I didn't have money in my pocket, but I had something even better in my heart. I had the satisfaction that I had helped out someone in need, and that was a great feeling.

LESSON LEARNED: There are bigger rewards in life than money.

THINK ABOUT THIS: Have you ever done a good deed for somebody without asking for anything in return? How did it make you feel? Can you try to do one thing every week that will make a difference in another person's life?

KID'S CORNER

Kids like you talk about their own business (ad)ventures.

Zack Soenen, age 9

Someday, I hope to start a video game tournament for kids only. It would be in my basement. Kids would pay $3.50 to get in, and the winner of the tournament would get half the money. The tournaments would be held once every month. Each month would be a different game.

LESSON LEARNED: You can have fun making money!

THINGS TO THINK ABOUT . . .

Even if you fail, it's the trying that counts

My parents taught me this lesson and it's one that I've always followed.

Think about it—if I'd never tried anything because I was afraid to fail, I wouldn't have started my very first business—and I wouldn't be where I am today!

I'm the first to admit that all of my ideas aren't good ones. And they aren't always successful. One time I failed at a T-shirt business (see the following story), but I learned a valuable lesson. I needed to do research for my next project and "look before I leaped."

So when you really think about it, no attempt at success is a complete washout. Even when you fail, you can gain something very important—knowledge. And as long as you try your hardest, you should never feel embarrassed about failing.

T-SHIRT TRAUMA

I spent a lot of time sitting in the bleachers, watching my older sisters play sports. My sister Beth is seven years older than me. She played on her high school volleyball team and boy, were they good! I went to almost every single one of Beth's games with my parents and other sisters.

During her senior year in high school, we all began to realize that Beth's team was destined to make it to the state championships. That was when I started planning my next venture. . . .

I knew if the team—the Providence Celtics—made it to the state championship, a lot of fans would be there cheering them on. What better way to distinguish the Celtic fans from the others than by having them all wear the same T-shirts during the games?

I quickly designed a T-shirt that I could sell at the state games. Then I asked my mom and dad for help. I needed them to be investors in my T-shirt business!

They loaned me some money to print the T-shirts, and I added the money I had saved up from my previous jobs. I had a hundred T-shirts made in the school colors and couldn't wait for the big day when I could sell the shirts for a profit.

The day of the big game, my family arrived early. I had my box of T-shirts all ready. I created signs and had my entire family wear the shirts at the game. (I thought that would be great advertising.) I was so excited!

Needless to say, I was surprised when I walked into the gym and saw a whole bunch of people wearing T-shirts almost identical to the one's I'd made. *What is going on?* I thought. After asking a few people, I found out that the pep group at the high school had sold T-shirts *they* created—the week before the game! Almost everyone had one on.

"Oh no, what am I going to do now?" I asked my parents. They advised me to try to make the best of the situation, and that is what I did.

I marked the price of the shirts down low enough to cover the money I'd spent on them—and to ensure that I wouldn't be going home with a hundred Celtic volleyball shirts! Luckily, the shirts were so cheap, I was able to get rid of almost all of them.

In the end, I didn't make any money but didn't lose that much either. I also learned that I should do some research before starting up a business.

Which is exactly what I did the next time . . .

LESSON LEARNED: Even good ideas can flop. But even if your business doesn't turn out as you hoped, don't let it discourage you from moving on to other things.

THINK ABOUT THIS: Was there ever a time when things didn't turn out the way you had expected? Did you get discouraged? What, if anything, could you learn from that lesson and apply to your next venture?

Working with the Trump organization is a challenge, but no matter how hard things become, I never let it get me down.

KID'S CORNER

Kids like you talk about their own business (ad)ventures.

Mike Varga, age 10

If I was ever going to sell something, I would go to the store and buy Gatorade and chocolate chip cookies. I would go to the soccer field and set up a table to sell them to the boys and girls in the park. I would want to do that every Saturday. I would change the food every week. For example, I would sell Gatorade and cookies one week and Gatorade and chips the next. After three hours of selling I would go to the store and buy food for next week's sale.

LESSON LEARNED: It's important to make plans about the location and supplies for your business.

BRACELET BONANZA

One year, my mom and dad took us to New York for Christmas to spend a few days with my aunt and uncle.

I wasn't really excited about New York in December. I thought Disney World would be more fun. Things got worse when my aunt and my mom told me that we were going to the mall to go shopping. Ugh. I hated shopping!

Things were okay for about fifteen minutes. Then I started getting bored. I asked my mom if I could sit out on one of the benches by the fountain while they shopped in the store. She said okay, and I got out of there.

I was sitting on my bench plotting different escape routes from the mall when my eyes lighted on a group of six girls, all about my age, huddled around a cart where a vendor was selling jewelry. The girls were all very excited about something.

I walked over to get a closer look, pretending I was interested in the sunglasses, and overheard the tall girl say, "Oh my God! That is *so* beautiful!"

"How much is it?" a blond girl asked.

"Ten dollars," replied another, with freckles.

They oohed and aahed some more before they went on their way.

After they left, I put down the sunglasses and picked up one of the odd-looking string bracelets that they were making such a fuss over. *This is what they were going crazy about?* I asked myself.

As I walked back across the mall toward the store where my mom was shopping, I found myself glancing at the wrist of every girl passing. It was amazing! They were *all* wearing those same little bracelets.

Then it hit me. This was an opportunity!

I whirled around and ran back to the cart vendor. "I don't have ten dollars. And I live in Chicago. Do you know anywhere else I can buy this bracelet? It's for a friend of mine," I said.

The cart vendor smiled. He handed me his business card and said, "Here's the phone number for my shop. The bracelets are only six dollars if you buy over the phone. I can send them to you in Chicago."

"Perfect," I said as I walked back to the store. And that night, I told my dad about my idea.

"Dad, I can buy these bracelets for six dollars. If girls are buy-ing them for ten dollars, I could make *four dollars per bracelet*! Plus

I don't know *anyone* back home who wears these yet. I could sell them to every girl in the school! Can I borrow some money to order some?"

My dad wasn't sure. He thought it was a lot of money for such a simple bracelet. I could have given up right then, but I didn't. The next day at breakfast, I asked my mom, "Mom, can I borrow forty dollars?"

"Forty dollars?" she gasped. "What in heaven's name for?"

I told her my idea.

Mom wasn't sure the girls in Chicago would like the bracelets. What if they didn't buy them? But I *knew* they would buy them. There was no doubt in my mind.

I sat there, eating my Cheerios, wondering how I was going to get those bracelets.

My older sister Katie felt sorry for me and let me have all of the money in her bank. She said she liked my idea. But the amount of money she had wasn't enough.

She reminded me that our uncle Joe seemed to have a lot of money. He always gave us great presents for our birthdays.

She was right! Uncle Joe used to give us one-dollar bills just for running off to the fridge to get him a can of soda! So, that night, I shared my idea with Uncle Joe, and he said, "I believe in you, kid! Make it happen!" He gave me the money the next day.

The ten bracelets I ordered showed up at my house the next week. I took them to school, but when I showed them to Emily and Kim, they said the bracelets were "gross." I was shocked! I went home that night and told my sister Katie that it would probably be a long time till I could pay her back.

Although I was discouraged, I took the bracelets to school again the next day. I decided to give one of the bracelets to Ashley. Everyone always seemed to like Ashley's style, and she was very popular. I told Ashley the bracelet was from New York. She said thank you and that she liked it.

In the lunch line that day, I saw a group of girls huddled around Ashley. They were all making a huge fuss about something. As I walked past, I overheard Ashley say, "It's from New York." There were squeals of delight from the group.

Bingo!

By the end of the day, I'd sold the remaining nine bracelets. All ten bracelets were gone, and even though I gave one away for free, I had $54 of *profit* in my pocket!

LESSON LEARNED: If you know you're right, believe in your idea and surround yourself with people who believe in you too.

THINK ABOUT THIS: Did you ever have an idea that people laughed at? What if you hadn't listened to those people and kept on trying?

I liked getting new gadgets for Christmas. Especially ones that could help out with my businesses!

KID'S CORNER

Kids like you talk about their own business (ad)ventures.

Robert Morrow, age 10

I love Atomic Fireballs. They're a kind of candy that's red hot!

I used to buy my fireballs from the store every day after school, and so would all my classmates. Then one day, I went with my parents to a price club. There I found a whole big box of fireballs! When I looked at the price, I noticed that they were much cheaper than the fireballs I was buying. And they were the exact same thing!

I convinced my dad to buy the huge box of fireballs, and the next day after school, I sold them to my classmates for less than the local store charged. I still made a ton of money, and my friends got a better deal!

LESSON LEARNED: If you give your product a lower price, you'll sell more than the other guy.

WORDS OF WISDOM

Today's most successful people were once kids just like you. Check out their words of wisdom, and learn the secret to their success.

When I was in elementary school, my teacher told my class to build models of our homes in the sandbox. All my classmates built uncomplicated sand houses—all small, one story, and very simple. I built a castle.

My castle took up half of the sandbox and was almost as tall as me. My real house didn't look anything like that, of course. But the castle was the kind of house I dreamed of living in.

My friends loved my castle, but my teacher came out and scolded me. She told me that I didn't follow directions and that I hogged up the whole sandbox. I didn't get a good grade.

By the time the annual arts fair came around, my teacher decided that our project would be a sand model of our classroom. She put me in charge. Why? Because I had dared to dream big.

LESSON LEARNED: Dreams are important. They are inside all of us. Decide what your dream is, then believe in yourself in order to achieve it.

—Donny Deutsch
Chairman and CEO of New York City advertising firm
Deutsch, Inc. Host of CNBC's *The Big Idea with Donny Deutsch* and frequent guest on *The Apprentice*

By working hard and remembering all the lessons I learned, I ended up working with Donald Trump. If you do the same, you can make it big, too.

PART 2

---

20 Kid Businesses You Can Start Today!

Here are some business ideas that will get you started on the road to success. You can use them to make some of your own money, or as fundraisers for your school, your team or any other worthy cause!

Be sure a parent or responsible adult always knows where you are and who you're doing business with—then get ready to rake in some cash!

Kid Business #1
POOL-CLEANING BUSINESS

Lots of people love swimming in the summer, but caring for a pool is a lot of work. Many adults don't have time to take care of their pools the way they'd like. That's where you come in.

As a *pool cleaner*, you will be expected to skim the surface of your clients' pools, vacuum the bottoms, and add chemicals to the water to keep it sparkling clean.

PROS AND CONS

Cons	Pros
Business is seasonal if you live in a northern town. You'll only make money in the summertime.	Business is outdoors. You'll never miss out on a nice summer day.
Pool chemicals can be expensive, and hazardous if not handled correctly.	If you don't have a pool of your own, you still get to cool off in the hot sun.

This business is good for you if:
- You like water and can swim
- You live in a warm climate
- You are at least twelve years old

This business is bad for you if:
- You can't swim
- You have sensitive skin that could react badly to harsh chemicals or constant sunlight
- Your family goes on vacation every summer

FIVE TIPS FOR GETTING YOUR POOL-CLEANING BUSINESS STARTED

1. Pass out flyers to neighbors who have pools.

2. Stake out stores that sell pool supplies. Hand out flyers to customers or post flyers near the entrance.

3. Work with each client individually the first time so you know their specific needs and expectations.

4. Establish whether you will use your client's supplies or bring your own.

5. Try to book a number of standing appointments with your clients (For example, agree that you'll clean the pool once a week—every Monday at 3 p.m.—for two months.) The cash will start rolling in!

Kid Business #2
HOMEWORK HELPER

Many boys and girls like to play school when they're little. As a *homework helper*, you can be a teacher for real. Not only will you make money, you'll have the good feeling that comes from knowing that you really helped someone.

You'll be expected to help with homework after school or on weekends. You can either follow along with your client's lessons or come up with your own interesting ways to aid in learning.

PROS AND CONS

Cons

This is a business that needs to be conducted after school on weekends, so your free time will be limited.

You must keep a strict schedule. Your "students" are counting on you!

Pros

You get to work with a subject or subjects you enjoy and are good at.

It is very rewarding to see your "student" gain self confidence in a subject that was once hard for him or her.

This business is good for you if:
- You like to share your knowledge with others
- You like to work with kids younger than you
- You have the patience to explain and demonstrate information until the kid "gets" it
- You are creative in teaching the understanding of a subject/subjects

This business is bad for you if:
- You don't like school
- You know you don't have a lot of patience when someone doesn't "understand" something you try to tell them
- Your own homework doesn't leave you with enough free time to help someone else

FIVE TIPS TO GET YOUR HOMEWORK-HELPER BUSINESS STARTED

1. Make up a flyer and give it to teachers in lower grades. They can refer you to parents of students who are struggling.

2. List your recent and current teachers as references on your flyer. Parents will want to check on your grades and reliability.

3. List subjects you could assist in. For example, reading, reviewing homework, math problems, school projects, etc.

4. Create progress reports for the parents.

5. Try to think of activities to make learning fun.

I love tutoring. I've always loved it. Maybe that's because it's in my genes. Here's a photo of me graduating from college, with my mom, a school principal, and my dad, a college professor, at my side.

Kid Business #3
SUDS FOR SPOT!

Dogs are tons of fun. Starting a dog-washing business is a great way to earn extra money while having a ball with man's best friend!

As a *dog washer* you'll be responsible for thoroughly washing all types of dogs. You might also be expected to dry them and brush them until their hair is tangle-free.

PROS AND CONS

Cons
You'll get wet.

You may get scratched or even nipped at by a nervous dog.

Some dogs will require a lot of time and patience to wash properly.

Pros
Not a lot of setup is required.

Supplies are inexpensive, which means your profits will be bigger than with other businesses.

You get to work with all types of dogs and play with them.

This business is good for you if:
- You like dogs and know how to handle them
- You don't mind getting wet and soapy
- You don't have a lot of cash to start up a new business

This business is bad for you if:
- You're allergic to or afraid of dogs
- You live in a pet-free apartment building
- You don't like to get messy

FIVE TIPS TO GET YOUR SUDS-FOR-SPOT BUSINESS STARTED

1. Begin by getting supplies: shampoo, old towels, and water.

2. Don't forget doggie treats.

3. At least one day before the dog wash, set up posters in places you know dogs and their owners hang out—like the dog run at your local park.

4. Start by cleaning your own dog or a neighbor's dog so future customers can see what a great job you do.

5. Encourage repeat business! Create a sign to let customers know that you'll be washing dogs every week. (For example, your sign could say, DOG WASH EVERY TUESDAY FROM 10 TO 12.) That way, your customers will know where and when to return.

I started a pet-cleaning business when I was a kid. My first client was my dog, Muffin.

Kid Business #4
TECHNOLOGY TUTOR

Ever feel like you know more about computers and electronics than your parents or grandparents? Chances are you do!

Use your knowledge to help the less tech-savvy learn word processing, e-mail, instant messaging, or to use the Internet! If you're good with electronics, you can also help people learn to program and use their new DVD or MP3 players!

As a *technology tutor*, you'll be expected to demonstrate how to use a computer to a beginner and, perhaps, tackle more advanced programs for your "students" who are ready for adventure in the world of technology. You may also need to be familiar with how different electronic devices work.

PROS AND CONS

Cons

Your students may get frustrated when they don't understand something.

This is an indoor job, which means you may miss out on sunny days.

You may have to do a lot of research and reading to gain as much knowledge as possible about the programs and electronics you'll use.

Pros

No start-up costs. All you need is your brainpower and a few flyers!

It's rewarding to teach somebody something you're a pro at.

This is a year-round business—good for any kind of weather.

This business is good for you if:
- You know a lot about computers and electronics and are naturally good at using them
- You like to share what you know
- You enjoy working with people

This business is bad for you if:
- You love spending time outdoors.
- You're not patient with people
- You're all thumbs around computers or other electronics

FIVE TIPS TO GET YOUR TECHNOLOGY-TUTOR BUSINESS STARTED

1. Post notices about your business in places like retirement homes.

2. Put together a portfolio of programs that you know and attach samples.

3. Establish a fee—you'll want to charge per half hour or per one-hour session.

4. Have a tech-support hotline that clients can call if they don't remember their lessons or aren't sure what to do.

5. Offer package deals for a discount! For example, if three half-hour lessons normally cost fifteen dollars, charge twelve dollars if the customer books all three lessons in advance.

Kid Business #5
IT'S PARTY TIME!

At a birthday party full of preschoolers, moms need extra help entertaining and corralling the party guests. As a *birthday party coordinator*, you'll help do just that!

As part of your service, you can plan games and activities for children's house parties, watch the kids, help serve the cake and other food, help make and pass out goodie bags, and help moms clean up after the party.

PROS AND CONS

Cons

If you don't know many families with small children, you may have a hard time finding customers.

A roomful of small kids = craziness. You'll be working in loud, chaotic conditions.

The kids might not listen to you.

Pros

If you're a creative person, you can put your brain to work thinking up new games, party themes, and activities for your clients.

If you're good at your job, other moms at the party will notice. You may get additional jobs as a result of your work.

This job is good for you if:
- You like children and have experience watching them
- You're creative
- You're organized and responsible

This job is bad for you if:
- You would rather *be* at the party than *help* at the party
- You don't have patience with small kids
- You're easily distracted

FIVE TIPS TO GET YOUR BIRTHDAY-PARTY-COORDINATING BUSINESS STARTED

1. Do some research! Read magazine articles and books about kids' parties to inspire you and get your creative juices flowing.

2. Create flyers to advertise your business. Put them in playgrounds and around local toy stores.

3. On your flyer, offer a discount to your first five customers. That will really get the business rolling!

4. Offer different packages of services for different age groups. For example, the things you'll do for a six-year-old's party should be different from the things you'll do for a two-year-old's.

5. Supply references to moms from parents of other kids whose parties you've worked on.

Kid Business #6
KID COACH

When I was younger, we didn't start playing organized sports until almost seventh grade. Now kids can join the soccer team when they're just four years old!

Becoming a one-on-one *sports coach* involves working with kids on a sport of their choice. It may involve throwing pitches, kicking a soccer ball, or shooting free throws.

PROS AND CONS

Cons

Coaching someone who isn't a natural athlete may be frustrating and tedious.

For some sports, you'll need to practice outdoors. A rainy week could wash out your profits.

Pros

You'll get to earn money doing something you love—playing sports!

You will feel a sense of accomplishment as you watch someone gain in confidence and skill because of you.

All you need are some flyers and your natural ability.

This business is good for you if:
- You love sports and are talented in a few different ones
- You like working with little kids
- You have been playing sports for a long time

This business is bad for you if:
- You don't have experience in sports
- You don't like to play outdoors
- You don't have a lot of patience with little kids

FIVE TIPS TO GET YOUR SPORTS-COACHING BUSINESS STARTED

1. Create a routine of warm-ups, drills, and a cooldown for each sport you'd like to coach. Make sure the routine isn't too tough for younger kids—remember, they're just beginners.

2. Attend games of your or your friends' younger siblings. Post flyers at the games advertising your business.

3. Post flyers near stores that sell athletics equipment.

4. Offer to create a chart to showing how your "athletes" are improving. For example, you could chart that on your first day of coaching, a child made ten out of forty free throws—and after one month of coaching, he or she made thirty out of forty free throws.

5. Be positive. Let your clients know you believe in them, and watch them achieve!

Everyone needs a bit of coaching now and then. Here's a picture of me with Greg Cuneo, my coach and mentor.

Kid Business #7
CAR WASH AND WAX

People use their cars *a lot*. As a result, they get dirty. To protect them from outside elements, cars need to be cleaned and waxed regularly. Sometimes parents don't have time. So grab a sponge and a bucket and get ready to go to work at a *car-wash-and-wax* business!

PROS AND CONS

Cons

This is a seasonal business if you live in a northern state.
Rainy days will cut down on the amount of business you get.

Car-safe cleaners and waxes can be expensive, but you'll need them if you want to do the job right.

Lots of soap and water can irritate your hands.

Pros

If you can't get to the pool or beach, this is a great way to cool off on a hot summer day.

This is a great business to start with a group of friends. You'll get through more cars that way, and you'll get to have fun while you work!

This business is good for you if:
- You enjoy working outside
- You can pay attention to detail
- You can handle hard work and want to build some muscle

This business is bad for you if:
- You don't like manual labor
- You'd rather hang out indoors

FIVE TIPS TO GET YOUR CAR-WASH-AND-WAX BUSINESS STARTED

1. Purchase supplies like tire cleaner/shiner, wax, and car-safe cleaning agents. Ask to borrow your parents' handheld vacuum.

2. Offer an array of services. Lots of things need to be cleaned in a car. Make a price sheet with all of your services so clients can check off what they would like done. Some services include wash, wax, tire shining, and vacuuming the interior.

3. Indicate to all your customers that the cars will be hand-washed. This is far better for the car's paint than machine washing.

4. Create a large sign you can set up while you are washing cars so people driving by can see you hard at work and ask you to wash their car.

5. Stay on the job and don't "goof off" with your friends until the job is done. You'll feel good about the job you did, and so will your customer!

Kid Business #8
HOW DOES YOUR GARDEN GROW?

Every home owner wants a green, flowering garden. But it's a lot of work to plant flowers and bulbs each season. Older home owners (or super-busy ones) might not be able to keep up their gardens the way they'd like.

By starting up this *gardening* business, your job would be to help the home owner plant different "in-season" flowers or bulbs, pull weeds, and water.

PROS AND CONS

Cons

If you're not strong, your arms might get sore from all the digging and pulling.

This work is messy!

Pros

You get to see the results of your hard work when the flowers start to bloom.

You can enjoy nature and the great outdoors.

This business is good for you if:
- You like flowers and plants
- You think getting dirty is fun!
- You can pay attention and listen to the instructions of your clients

This business is bad for you if:
- You're allergic to flowers or plants
- You like being neat at all times
- You're sensitive to sun, fertilizer, or *worms*!

FIVE TIPS TO GET YOUR GARDENING BUSINESS STARTED

1. Create a flyer and pass it out to your neighbors in the spring and fall, when people think most about gardening.

2. Gather some basic gardening tools (like a hand rake, a trowel, and gloves).

3. Look up planting on the Internet and learn the basics of outdoor plant care.

4. Offer different packages to your clients—from onetime help with planting to weekly garden maintenance.

5. Help your parents with their own garden so that potential clients can get a look at your great work!

Kid Business #9
MAKING MEMORIES

Everyone loves to take pictures, but what do you with them after they're printed? Some people end up with boxes and boxes of unorganized pictures. That's where you, super–*scrapbook maker*, come to the rescue!

It takes lots of creativity and organization to turn a bunch of jumbled photos into a memory book that will bring your clients smiles for a lifetime. If you're at home with scissors and glue and have an eye for design, this could be the summer job for you!

PROS AND CONS

Cons

This business requires loads of concentration, sometimes for long periods.

In the summer, working indoors might not be the business for you.

Pros

You can set your own hours! Scrapbooking can happen anywhere, anytime—on the weekends or after school.

This business is good for you if:
- You like to be creative and artistic
- You have some experience with taking your own pictures and creating your own scrapbooks
- You enjoy organizing and sorting

This business is bad for you if:
- You would rather be active and outdoors
- You're all thumbs around craft supplies
- You only enjoy (sometimes) looking at someone else's albums

FIVE TIPS TO GET YOUR SCRAPBOOKING BUSINESS STARTED

1. Gather your supplies at a craft store. You'll need albums, stencils, scissors, paper, borders, glue, etc.

2. Create a fun and funky flyer showcasing your talent.

3. Post your flyer near day-care centers. Busy moms may be the most in need of your services!

4. Create a portfolio of what you have done. Start with on your own scrapbook to show off the kind of work you can do.

5. Work carefully and neatly—remember, you're working with your customer's treasured memories!

Kid Business #10
WRAP IT UP!

Holiday time is a busy time for everyone, but it's also a great time to make some cash! Start your own *gift-wrapping* business and you'll make lots of people jolly this holiday season!

You'll be expected to neatly wrap the gifts, decorate them with ribbons, and add a gift card.

PROS AND CONS

Cons	Pros
This is seasonal work. Sadly, the holidays only come once a year.	This is a good way to earn money for the holidays!
This can involve a lot of travel as you shuttle from one client's house to another.	You won't need to buy any supplies (your clients will provide the wrapping paper and bows).

This business is good for you if:
- You love the look of a nicely wrapped package
- You know how to wrap neatly
- You're only looking for some quick holiday cash and don't want a permanent job

This business is bad for you if:
- Your gifts look like they could have been wrapped by a three-year-old
- You're never full of holiday cheer
- You can't keep secrets and would spill the beans about the gifts you wrapped to the person who was to receive them

FIVE TIPS TO GET YOUR GIFT-WRAPPING BUSINESS STARTED

1. Stuff flyers in your neighbors' mailboxes in September. Many parents shop early!

2. Distribute flyers in mailboxes again the day after Thanksgiving and in early December for those who shop late.

3. Practice your gift-wrapping skills on empty boxes or on your own presents at home.

4. Go to a department store (with an adult) that has a gift-wrapping department and get some ideas.

5. Be neat and always clean up your work area when you finish the job for the day. That way, you're sure to be asked back next year!

Kid Business #11
SAFE AT HOME

When families go on vacation, they like to know everything at their house will be safe and sound. As a *house checker*, your job is to keep things up at your clients' house while they're away. This includes tasks like watering outdoor and indoor plants, taking in the mail, feeding pets, and making sure no packages or newspapers are left on the porch or in front of the house.

PROS AND CONS

Cons

You need to find families living near you who are going on vacation. Jobs may be few and far between.

It's just you and an empty house. The work can get kind of lonely.

Pros

You may have repeat customers from year to year.

You can work during the summer, spring break, and other holidays.

You can do the job according to your schedule—as long as you do it.

This business is good for you if:
- Your family doesn't go on a lot of vacations and you're around to do the jobs
- You're very responsible and won't flake out on your duties

This business is bad for you if:
- You would like to work more hours than this job can provide
- You would like steady pay
- You go on vacation with your family quite a bit

FIVE TIPS TO GET YOUR HOUSE-CHECKING BUSINESS STARTED

1. Create business cards on the computer and pass them out to friends, family, and neighbors.

2. Build your reputation for being reliable and on-the-job. The word will spread.

3. Be courteous and polite when speaking with potential customers.

4. Promise your clients a full report of just what you did each day they were away.

5. Do a little something extra for each client—like leaving a welcome-home note or little present for when they return!

Kid Business #12
TAKE A WALK!

When I was growing up, a lot of people in my neighborhood had one or more dogs. In many cases, the dog owners worked full-time jobs and couldn't let the dogs out during the day. As a *dog walker*, you'll give those four-legged friends some exercise!

This job involves walking the dog or dogs and cleaning up after them.

PROS AND CONS

Cons
The dogs will need to be taken care of in all types of weather. This includes rainy and snowy days.

You'll need to clean up after the dogs—in other words, "scoop the poop."

Pros
This job gives you the opportunity to walk and play with all types of dogs.

You'll get a lot of exercise.

You'll make your furry friends very, very, happy.

This job is good for you if:
- You like dogs
- You like being outdoors
- You like exercise, especially walking

This business is bad for you if:
- You're allergic to dogs
- You're afraid of dogs
- You don't like rain, heat, or snow

FIVE TIPS TO GET YOUR DOG-WALKING BUSINESS STARTED

1. Create a flyer that will advertise your business and put it near dog runs and pet stores.

2. Make a T-shirt advertising your business that you can wear while you're walking the dogs. The T-shirt could say, PROFESSIONAL DOG WALKER. That way, people on the street can stop and ask you about your business.

3. Create a list of clients to use as references.

4. Give your furry friends an owner-approved treat at the end of each walk.

5. Have fun with your clients (dogs)! They will love you in return.

Kid Business #13
MOTHER'S HELPER

Most moms can use an extra set of hands to help out around the house. As a *mother's helper* you'll be responsible for assisting mothers with light chores like folding clothes, dusting, and vacuuming. The job may also include:

- Playing games with the children
- Helping to feed small children
- Taking kids for walks around the neighborhood

PROS AND CONS

Cons	Pros
This job will keep you very, very busy.	This is excellent preparation for babysitting.
The work is intense and tiring.	You'll be supervised on the job, so it's like being an apprentice!

This business is good for you if:
- You like working with children
- You're not old enough to babysit—yet
- You take orders well
- You like to help out your mom doing chores around the house
- You have younger brothers and sisters to practice on

This business is bad for you if:
- You don't like working with small children
- You are messy and don't like to clean up after yourself, let alone other people
- You don't have a lot of patience

FIVE TIPS TO GET YOUR MOTHER'S-HELPER BUSINESS STARTED

1. Ask some of the moms in the neighborhood if you can help them out for an hour free of charge.

2. Create a list of things you will do as a mother's helper and the days and times you would like to work.

3. When you start this business, it's best to talk to future customers in person.

4. Tell them what you can do and just how you can help ease their work.

5. Your personality will get a lot of customers; your reliability will keep them.

Kid Business #14
DAY CAMP

If you like summer mornings, kids, and games, this is the business for you!

Busy moms would love an hour or two during the summer, when kids are on vacation, to get some household chores done— or just to have some "time off," knowing their kids are safe, in the neighborhood, and having fun.

As a *backyard "summer camp" organizer* you'll be expected to provide games and activities for small children in your backyard for an hour or two, two to three mornings per week.

PROS AND CONS

Cons

Sometimes small children can be cranky first thing in the morning.

If it's a rainy day, you'll have to cancel your camp day, and you won't get paid.

Pros

After working a couple of hours in the morning, you'll have the rest of your day free!

This is a good team business— one you can start with friends! For every three children that come to your camp, have one counselor.

This business is good for you if:
- You're old enough to babysit
- You like little kids
- You have a lot of patience
- You're kind and responsible

This business is bad for you if:
- You like to sleep late
- You have so many of your own activities that you can't commit to having the camp at least two or three mornings a week

FIVE TIPS TO GET YOUR BACKYARD "SUMMER CAMP" BUSINESS STARTED

1. Hand out flyers listing the games and activities provided at your backyard "summer camp."

2. List the age range of children you feel comfortable counseling and the times and days of the week camp will be in session.

3. Set up a safe, "kid-proof" area in the backyard where children can come for one or two hours, two to three times a week.

4. Organize age-appropriate games and activities for the children.

5. Provide snacks and juice or lemonade for the children at the end of each session (with each parent's permission).

Kid Business #15
GO, GO, GARAGE SALE!

Spring, summer, and fall are great times for people in the neighborhood to hold garage sales. As a *garage sale assistant*, your job is to keep your eyes and ears open for potential clients who need your assistance in conducting their garage sales.

How can you help run a garage sale? In most cases, you'll be expected to arrive at your client's house early in the morning to set things up and stay late to pack up, discard items, or put them away.

PROS AND CONS

Cons

This might be an all-day job in the summer or on a weekend, when you would have to give up free time.

Carrying boxes and arranging items can be hard, strenuous work.

Pros

This is a great business if you enjoy working with people.

You can improve your sales technique by demonstrating or displaying items.

This business is good for you if:
- You enjoy working with people
- You like to sell things
- You can follow directions and orders

This business is bad for you if:
- You're shy about talking to people and "selling" to them
- An all-day job is too long for you
- You would rather work alone

FIVE TIPS TO GET YOUR GARAGE-SALE-ASSISTANT BUSINESS STARTED

1. Start with friends and family. Ask if they'd like help with their garage sales, then use them as references for other clients.

2. Keep your eyes peeled for garage sale flyers around community bulletin boards!

3. List your services on a sheet to give to potential clients. For example, you may:
- Place stickers on items for pricing
- Keep a log of what is sold and for what amount
- Be on hand to keep an eye on things and answer any questions
- Take charge of the sale of any kid items, like toys
- Help with the cleanup after the sale is over

4. Offer your services for free to your first client.

5. Be helpful, and word will spread!

Kid Business #16
WEB SITE DEVELOPER

This may be one of the most profitable kid businesses around! If you are really tech savvy, consider being a *Web site creator* for other people—or local businesses!

Most Internet providers (like AOL) have tools for building your own basic site easily—so check them out! This might be the business for you!

PROS AND CONS

Cons	Pros
A business creating Web sites can be difficult and very time consuming if you don't have a lot of experience in this area.	This will give you great experience if you want to be in computers and create Web sites professionally someday.
You'll be spending a lot of time sitting at a computer.	Lots of adults need help creating a Web site. You can use your Web site business to show off your talents and knowledge in this area.

This business is good for you if:
- You're twelve or older
- You like working on computers
- You're creative
- You are very focused

This business is bad for you if:
- You aren't good with computers
- You would rather work outside at a job that involves more activity

FIVE TIPS TO GET YOUR WEB-SITE-CREATOR BUSINESS STARTED

1. Go to your Internet provider and check out their tools for creating a site. Play around with them—have fun!

2. Create a Web site that advertises your business and be sure to include information on how clients can contact you.

3. Pass out flyers that direct people to your Web site so they can see your work.

4. Place an ad in the local newspaper or church bulletin with the address of your site and a list of your services. Include in your advertisements a list of any classes you have taken that will help you in Web site development.

5. Include a reference from your computer teacher at school so people will know you're ready to do a great job!

Kid Business #17
GARAGE-CLEANING BUSINESS

Every family that has a garage knows how messy it can get. Between piling stuff inside and accidental spills, most people's garages could use a thorough cleaning at least once a year. But it's a big job, and few people want to take the time to do it.

Cleaning a garage might involve removing its entire contents, sweeping and hosing down the floor, and possibly scrubbing it with a strong cleaning solution.

Garage cleaning is a good business for a pair or a team. A discussion with the owner concerning which items should be replaced, discarded, or donated is necessary before you proceed.

PROS AND CONS

Cons	Pros
This is a dirty business.	You might pick up a good bargain in the "donate" pile.
It could require heavy manual labor.	Usually the financial reward is pretty good.
You have to split the money if you work with a team.	You get to work with a friend.

This business is good for you if:
- You're strong and don't mind hard work
- You're good at organizing
- You're at least twelve years old and can use chemicals to clean the garage floor

This business is bad for you if:
- You don't like to get dirty
- You don't like to get wet
- You're not an organized person

FIVE TIPS TO GET YOUR GARAGE-CLEANING BUSINESS STARTED

1. Clean your own garage! Take "before" and "after" photos and put them in a flyer you will pass out to your neighbors.

2. Pass out your flyers at the beginning of spring, when most people think about "spring cleaning."

3. Create a sign that you can display as you're working on your clients' garages. Give the name of your business and a way to contact you. When people see you hard at work on someone else's garage, they'll want to hire you too!

4. Walk through the garage with the client as he or she tells you just what is to be accomplished. Ask, "What do you want this garage to look like when I'm done?"

5. Keep a list of clients and call or contact them the following year to remind them, "It's time to clean the garage!"

Kid Business #18
LET IT SNOW, LET IT SNOW, LET IT SNOW!

Winters in Chicago, where I grew up, can be a lot of fun. My friends and I got to play in the snow, make forts and snowmen, and, best of all, wish for snow days!

But snowstorms can also cause big hassles. It can be difficult for cars to get in and out of driveways on a very snowy day. Neighbors may not have time to shovel their way out.

Snow shoveling is a strenuous job, but you can make a lot of money doing it.

PROS AND CONS

Cons	Pros
It can be tiring.	It's fun to be out in the snow.
Larger driveways can take a lot of time.	You can do this with a friend or two.
This won't be a steady job—you'll have to wait for snowstorms to make money.	

This business is good for you if:
- You live in a state where it snows a lot
- You like physical work

This business is bad for you if:
- You catch cold easily
- It doesn't snow much where you live
- You want a steady income

FIVE TIPS TO GET YOUR SNOW-SHOVELING BUSINESS STARTED

1. Buy a good shovel.

2. At the beginning of winter, pass out flyers that people can post on their refrigerators so they'll have your number handy.

3. Create a list of your prices for driveways, sidewalks, etc.

4. Ask a brother or sister or a friend who lives close by if they are willing to be your partner. You'll get more houses done that way, faster.

5. Listen to the weather forecast on your local station. If you hear that a snowstorm is coming, pass out another round of flyers to your neighbors. Be sure to include your phone number so they know how to reach you!

Kid Business #19
THE GRASS IS GREENER

If you live in the suburbs, in the summertime you're probably surrounded by green grass and flowers. Taking care of a lawn can be very time consuming. When I was younger, my dad had me mow the lawn, edge along the sidewalks and street, and trim around the flower beds. That was no small task.

Once I mastered my lawn, I took care of the lawns of some of my neighbors. Here's how you can get a *lawn-mowing* business started.

PROS AND CONS

Cons

This business is seasonal if you live in a northern town.

If you don't have any experience, you may need some training in how to operate the equipment.

Pros

You get to be outside enjoying nice summer days.

You don't have to spend much money to get this business started.

You can create a flexible schedule for yourself.

This business is good for you if:

- You know how to operate a lawn mower
- You live in the suburbs
- You like to be outside

This business is bad for you if:

- You need steady, year-round income
- You have seasonal allergies

FIVE TIPS TO GET YOUR LAWN-MOWING BUSINESS STARTED

1. Start your advertising in early March, before people hire other services.

2. Create a flyer. On the back, list all the services you'll provide, like trimming, edging, weed pulling, and watering the flowers.

3. Think about creating "package deals" for your services. For example, offer four weeks of lawn service at a slightly lower price than if a client bought each week individually.

4. Make up a T-shirt that you can wear while you're working. Print the name of your business on the shirt and list the phone number or contact information so people who see you hard at work can get in touch with you about their lawns.

5. Did you do any snow shoveling in the winter? Let your shoveling clients know that you'll be mowing in the spring!

Kid Business #20
IT'S A LITTLE FISHY

Have you ever found yourself in a doctor's or dentist's office, staring at a tank full of tropical fish swimming lazily through the water?

Lots of professional offices have fish tanks, and someone has to clean them. If you like aquariums, maybe the best person for the job is *you*! Maybe you should start your own *fish-tank-cleaning* business.

You'll need to do lots of research on the care and maintenance of freshwater fish before you start. Once you read up, you'll be expected to keep the fish in your clients' tanks healthy and the tank sparkling clean.

WARNING! Saltwater fish are very delicate (and expensive). Limit your business to freshwater fish to avoid any horrible mishaps.

PROS AND CONS

Cons

You'll need to develop expertise in caring for fish before you can begin this business.

Dirty fish tanks can be smelly.

You'll need transportation to make the rounds of the offices you service.

Pros

This is a year-round business. Rain or shine, you'll still have a job to do.

If you like fish, this will help you learn lot about them and their environment.

This business is good for you if:
- You already care for your own fish
- You like marine life and want to learn more about it
- You don't mind getting a little wet

This business is bad for you if:
- You're grossed out by a dirty fish tank
- You have no way of getting from one office to the next

FIVE TIPS TO GET YOUR FISH-TANK-CLEANING BUSINESS STARTED

1. Start with your own doctor or dentist. Offer to care for his or her tank for free for one month. Then if he or she likes your work, you can begin charging for it.

2. Make business cards and place them next to the tank of your first client. Your cards should have the name of your business, a phrase or two about your services, and a way to contact you to set up an appointment.

3. Lots of doctors have offices in the same building or area. Place a flyer or card under the door of any doctors' offices nearby. List your first client as a reference.

4. Talk to local pet store owners about your business. They might be able to direct you to lots of local businesses that have fish tanks.

5. You'll need supplies to properly care for a fish tank. Get a deal on yours by offering to place the name of the local pet store on your flyers in exchange for a discount on the materials you'll need.

PART 3

Build Your Own
Business Model

WHAT IS A BUSINESS MODEL AND WHY DO I NEED ONE?

Before you attempt to do anything big, you need to have a plan.

Whether it's scoring a goal against a tough competitor or getting your mom to let you stay up later, strategy is the key to success.

Starting a business is no different. Even the most powerful businesspeople write down a *business plan* before they take action. *Business plans* help you think about the materials you will need, the actions you should take, and the possible problems you could run into *before* you run into them.

So how do you write a business plan? Take a look at the example below. We created it using the tech-tutor-business idea from page 81.

The Company

Technology Tutors is a small business designed to help people learn computer programs.

The Service

Technology Tutors was created for the purpose of earning extra money while teaching others how to use the computer. This includes word-processing programs, e-mailing, instant messaging, and surfing and searching the Internet.

Customers and Market Analysis

There are four retirement homes in the area where grandparents would like to use the computer to keep in touch with their children and grandchildren.

There are adults in the area who are going back to work or school and need to learn word-processing programs or how to create presentations on the computer.

Marketing Strategy

Technology Tutors will market itself in various ways. One way is to distribute and post flyers at retirement homes, grocery stores, etc.

Another way is to place advertisements in local newspapers and church bulletins.

We will also create a fact sheet to give to possible clients, listing all of the services we provide.

Technology Tutors will charge by the hour at a preset fee. This charge will be ten dollars, which is much lower than the sixty-dollar-per-hour fee that is charged by professional companies.

Start-up Costs

This is a low-cost business.

The only costs involved are for the paper used to create the flyers and for ad space bought in newspapers.

Your Business Plan!

Now it's your turn! Fill out the business plan on the next four pages before your start your own kid business. We've given you two blank forms in case you change your mind, make a mistake, or want to start more than one business.

The Company

(Explain here in one sentence what your company will do. You can include the name of your company if you've come up with one.)

_____

_____

_____

_____

The Service

(Here you can go into more detail about the products or services your company will provide.)

_____

_____

_____

_____

_____

_____

_____

Customers and Market Analysis

(Write here about how you think your business will make money. How do you know you'll have enough customers? Have you noticed any other, similar businesses in your area? Explain here why your business is different and/or better.)

_____

_____

_____

_____

_____

_____

Marketing Strategy

(Write down the things you'll do to make people aware of your business. Will you post flyers? Advertise? Create a fact sheet listing all the services you'll provide?)

_____

_____

_____

_____

_____

Start-up Costs

(Talk here about the things you need to start your business that will cost money.)

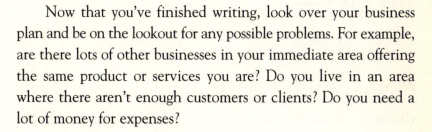

Now that you've finished writing, look over your business plan and be on the lookout for any possible problems. For example, are there lots of other businesses in your immediate area offering the same product or services you are? Do you live in an area where there aren't enough customers or clients? Do you need a lot of money for expenses?

Work those problems out now—*before* you open your kid business—and you'll have a greater chance of success!

The Company

(Explain here in one sentence what your company will do. You can include the name of your company if you've come up with one.)

_____

_____

_____

_____

The Service

(Here you can go into more detail about the products or services your company will provide.)

_____

_____

_____

_____

_____

_____

_____

Customers and Market Analysis

(Write here about how you think your business will make money. How do you know you'll have enough customers? Have you noticed any other, similar businesses in your area? Explain here why your business is different and/or better.)

_____

_____

_____

_____

_____

_____

Marketing Strategy

(Write down the things you'll do to make people aware of your business. Will you post flyers? Advertise? Create a fact sheet listing all the services you'll provide?)

_____

_____

_____

_____

_____

Start-up Costs

(Talk here about the things you need to start your business that will cost money.)

_____

_____

_____

_____

_____

Now that you've finished writing, look over your business plan and be on the lookout for any possible problems. For example, are there lots of other businesses in your immediate area offering the same product or services you are? Do you live in an area where there aren't enough customers or clients? Do you need a lot of money for expenses?

Work those problems out now—*before* you open your kid business—and you'll have a greater chance of success!

PART 4

Managing
Your Money

WHAT TO DO WITH YOUR MONEY

So you started a business and, hopefully, you made a profit! The next step is figuring out what to do with your money. After I made my first profits—from Grandma Rancic's pancakes—I put the money under my mattress.

Although the money was safe, I soon learned that there were much better places to put my profits. Places that might help my profits grow!

Part of "making it big" is learning how to manage your money. By this I mean coming up with a plan for how to spend it, save it, or, even better, *invest* it.

You don't have to make millions to start thinking about what to do with your money. Here are some ideas you may want to consider right now.

1. Pay Off Your Debts

Sometimes you need to borrow money to get your business started. Often you'll have to buy things, like paper for flyers or supplies, before you ever see a customer.

For example, if you start a dog-washing business, you'll need to buy dog shampoo, buckets, and dog treats. If you start a pool-cleaning business, you may need to buy chemicals to keep the pool clean. In the business world, the money you spend on these items is known as the "start-up cost."

Where do you get the funding for start-up costs? You either use money you have already saved or do what a lot of business owners do—take out a *loan*. Loans usually come from a bank, but they can also come from investors or friends and family.

When you're given money as part of a loan, you owe that money to the bank or to whoever lent it to you. When you owe someone else money, it's called a *debt*.

Debts usually build up *interest*, meaning that whoever lent you the money charges you *more* money—on top of what you already borrowed—for each month (or year) you don't pay the debt back.

How does that work? Let's say you borrow money to start a business. If you are loaned $200 to buy supplies and your loan comes with a 5 percent yearly interest rate, you end up paying 5 percent more money for every year you have the loan.

In the first year, you'll owe an extra $10.
5% of $200 = $10
$10 + $200 = $210

In the second year, you'll owe another $10 and 50 cents.
5% of $210 = $10.50
$10.50 + $210 = $220.50

In the third year, you'll owe another $11 on top of that!
5% of $220.50 = $11.03
$11.03 + 220.50 = 231.53

As you can see, if you don't pay your loan back quickly, your debt can grow and grow—making it harder and harder for you to pay it back.

If you let things go too long, you can end up deep, deep, deep in debt! This is why it's important to pay back any money you borrowed *before* you do anything else.

Even if you aren't charged interest on your loan—by your parents or whoever lends you money for start-up costs—it's good business practice to pay off debts *right away*.

Many adults make the mistake of not paying back money they borrowed as soon as possible. They end up having to pay large sums in interest. This causes them to get further and further into debt. Sometimes this even causes people to file for bankruptcy!

2. Put Your Money in the Bank

In the last section, we talked about the interest that builds up on a loan. That's the bad kind of interest. But there's also a good kind of interest—the kind that is paid *to* you.

Who gives you interest? The bank does when you put your money into certain kinds of *bank accounts*.

Some bank accounts earn interest. Others don't, but they do keep your money safe—much safer than in its hiding place under my mattress. Nowadays I keep a good deal of my money in a bank.

For you to do the same, you'll need a parent to take you to the bank to help you open an account. The amount of money you have and how long you want to keep it in the bank will help you decide what kind of account you should open. Also, be sure to ask about any fees that the bank charges on their accounts. Fees can zap money out of your pocket, so you'll want to find accounts with as few fees as possible. There are several accounts you should think about putting your money in. Here are a few:

Savings Accounts

This type of account usually earns you a small amount of interest (the good kind of interest that we talked about earlier—the kind that the bank pays *you*).

The interest you earn is always a *percentage*, or a portion, of the amount of money you keep in your account. This money is called your *balance*.

For example, if you have a *balance of $1,000.00* in your savings account and the *bank pays 2% interest*, you'll earn an extra *$20.00 per year in interest*. That's $20 that the bank just *gives* you!

Savings accounts are good to set up if you have money you won't need for a while— money you want to save. If you do need the money, you can *withdraw* it (take it out) from your account, but the longer your money stays in a savings account, the more interest you'll make.

The risk of losing any money you put in a savings account is very low since the bank guarantees that the amount you put in will be there until you want to take it out.

Money Market Accounts

If you've saved a good amount of money, usually over $1,000, you might consider a money market account instead of a standard savings account.

A money market account typically requires a *minimum balance*. This means you *have to* keep a certain amount of money in the account *at all times*. This minimum balance could be anywhere from $1,000 to $2,500.

In exchange for keeping a lot of cash in the account at all times, the bank will pay you a *higher interest rate* on your money. Today that may be around 3.5 percent a year, which is definitely more than the 2 percent you'll earn from a savings account.

The risk is also low that you'll lose any money you put in a money market account. And any money you put into a money market account *above* the minimum balance can be *withdrawn* (taken out of the bank) whenever you like.

Certificates of Deposit

CDs can earn you *even more interest* than money markets. The reason is that you can't take the money out anytime you want. With a CD, you agree not to touch the money for a set period.

Depending on the CD, that can be six months, twelve months, five years, or longer.

The longer you promise not to touch the money, the higher the interest rate the bank will give you. The risk of losing the money you put into a CD is similar to that of a money market account. Very low.

Checking Account

Have you ever seen your parents write checks?

When I was younger, I thought it was cool to fill out checks for my parents. But checks aren't just pieces of paper. They're part of a special kind of account.

A checking account is the kind of account you set up if you want your money to be available to you at all times. A checking account allows you to deposit (put in) and withdraw (take out) money quickly and easily.

When you need to pay for something, you can write a check for it, and the amount on the check will be taken out of the account. Or you can use an ATM card to take cash out of an ATM machine.

A checking account usually doesn't earn you interest, so you don't want to keep large amounts of money in there. But it's a safer place to keep your money than under your mattress, and it's still easy to use the money to buy things when you need to.

3. Invest!

Investing is another thing you can do with money you earned from your business. When you invest in something, that means you put your money into it in the hope that you'll get more money in return someday, when the value of that thing increases.

You can invest in a lot of things, especially when you're an adult! You can invest all of your money or just a *part* of it. (I keep some of my money in the bank—and some of my money in investments.)

There are many types of investments, but here are a few of the more common ones:

Stocks

You're giving your money to a large company so it can grow its business. This is called "buying a stock."

Once you buy a stock, you cross your fingers and hope that the company you invested in does well. In other words, that it sells a lot of its products or services, that it doesn't spend too much money, and that it *makes* a lot of money, too.

When all of that happens, the *value* of that company's stock goes up. And when it does, you can *sell* the stock that you bought for a higher price than you paid for it. When you do that, you make a profit!

For example, if you were one of the first kids to discover

Beanie Babies, before kids everywhere were crazy for them, you could have bought stock in the company that *makes* Beanie Babies.

Let's say you bought 100 shares of Beanie Babies stock and it cost $2 per share. You would have invested $200 in Beanie Babies, right? (100 shares x $2 per share = $200.)

Then, when kids everywhere went crazy for Beanie Babies, buying them up all over the world, the company made *a lot* of money. Because of that, the cost of Beanie Babies stock rose. Let's say, from the $2 you purchased it at to about $10 per share.

If you then *sold* your 100 shares of Beanie Babies stock at the price of $10 per share, you'd get $1,000 back. (100 shares x $10 per share = $1,000.)

And you'd have made $800 in profit! That's called putting your money to work.

CAUTION: A very big risk goes along with investing in stocks. It is *not* guaranteed that the company you choose will do well. And if that happens, you can actually *lose* the money that you invested. That's why even adults have to be very, very careful when they invest in the stock market.

Note: You'll need your parents to invest in stocks for you, because you must be at least eighteen to invest in the stock market.

Mutual Funds

Why? Because instead of buying shares in just one company, mutual funds buy stock in *many different* companies.

For example, if you put that $200 you invested above in Beanie Babies into a mutual fund, parts of that $200 could be invested in over 100 companies!

Some of these companies will do well, and their stock price will rise. Some of these companies will do poorly, and their stock price will fall. With a mutual fund, your hope is that successful companies will not only balance out the unsuccessful ones, but outweigh them—netting you a hefty profit!

This makes mutual funds less risky than stocks, but there's still an element of risk—especially if more of the stocks in your fund perform poorly than those that don't.

Note: You'll also need your parents to invest in a mutual fund for you. You must be eighteen before you can do it yourself.

Real Estate

Some people invest in *real estate*—otherwise known as *land*. If you can buy land that you think someday in the future will be worth a lot more money than you have to pay for it, you can buy it today and sell it in the future at a higher price. You keep the profits!

The trick here is to be as sure as you can that the land's value will increase in price instead of decrease.

Real estate investment is how Donald Trump made his fortune, and I do some real estate investing myself. Real estate investments are usually *very* costly, though. You'll really have to "make it big" before you can buy land.

Venture Investing

Sometimes you can use your profits to invest in small companies that are just starting out—the same way people invested in your business when *you* started. This is called *venture investing*.

Venture investing can be risky. If the business you invest in fails, you lose all the money you invested. But if the business does well, you can make money too!

For example, if you have $100 and your friend or someone else you know is starting a business, you may want to invest part of your money in that business—if you believe that business will be successful. For example, if you give your friend $25 to buy supplies for his business, that is venture investing.

An important part of venture investing is setting up an agreement or contract. A contract will state the amount of money you have invested and how much of the profits you will earn back once your friend's business starts making money. Be sure to agree to the terms of your investment before money changes hands. Otherwise, you could end up getting into a terrible disagreement about it later.

4. Grow Your Own Business

If your business is successful and you want to keep it going, you may want to use some of your profits to grow your business. You can ask your friends to be paid employees so you can provide services to more customers than you can handle on your own. Or you can take out an ad in a local paper to let more people know about your business.

In a way, this is just another kind of investment—an investment in yourself!

5. Buy Cool Stuff

This is definitely a fun thing to do with your money. One of the rewards of working hard is the freedom to buy things that you enjoy or, better yet, gifts for friends, family, and employees to make *them* happy.

6. Help Others

Sometimes the best reward for working hard is sharing your success and happiness with people who are less fortunate. Giving some of your profits to charity—and knowing that your work made a real difference in someone else's life—can make you very, very happy.

I know, because I give money (and also volunteer my time) to charities all across the country. In fact, I'm giving the profits I make from *this book* to charity too! Do you know of any charities that you would like to donate money to? If not, here are some you might want to consider. You can look them up on the Web and even donate money online (with some help from your parents)!

1. Alex's Lemonade Stand

2. The Pediatric Cancer Foundation

3. The American Red Cross

4. Elizabeth Glaser Pediatric AIDS Foundation

5. UNICEF (the United Nations Children's Fund)

6. The Juvenile Diabetes Foundation

PART 5

Your Contacts and Appointments

APPOINTMENTS

List your appointments here and never lose track of your commitments!

Client	Day	Time	Other Info

Client	Day	Time	Other Info

Client	Day	Time	Other Info

Client	Day	Time	Other Info

CONTACTS

Your contacts are the most important things you have in business. Past clients can become future ones. They can also refer their friends to you and your business. Other contacts can help you when you're confused and need some good advice.

Write all your contacts here to be sure to keep them safe and sound! I've started you off with one I hope you'll use. I'd love to hear from you about your business adventures!

Name: ___Bill Rancic___

Relationship (circle one): Client   Friend   (Adviser)   Partner   Investor

Contact info (address, e-mail, phone number):

___Bill@BillRancic.com___

Name: _____

Relationship (circle one): Client   Friend   Adviser   Partner   Investor

Contact info (address, e-mail, phone number):

_____

_____

_____

Name: _____

Relationship (circle one)**:** Client   Friend   Adviser   Partner   Investor

Contact info (address, e-mail, phone number)**:**

_____

_____

_____

Name: _____

Relationship (circle one)**:** Client   Friend   Adviser   Partner   Investor

Contact info (address, e-mail, phone number)**:**

_____

_____

_____

Name: _____

Relationship (circle one)**:** Client   Friend   Adviser   Partner   Investor

Contact info (address, e-mail, phone number)**:**

_____

_____

_____

Name: _____

Relationship (circle one): Client   Friend   Adviser   Partner   Investor

Contact info (address, e-mail, phone number):

_____

_____

_____

Name: _____

Relationship (circle one): Client   Friend   Adviser   Partner   Investor

Contact info (address, e-mail, phone number):

_____

_____

_____

Name: _____

Relationship (circle one): Client   Friend   Adviser   Partner   Investor

Contact info (address, e-mail, phone number):

_____

_____

_____

Name: _____

Relationship (circle one): Client   Friend   Adviser   Partner   Investor

Contact info (address, e-mail, phone number):

_____

_____

_____

Name: _____

Relationship (circle one): Client   Friend   Adviser   Partner   Investor

Contact info (address, e-mail, phone number):

_____

_____

_____

Name: _____

Relationship (circle one): Client   Friend   Adviser   Partner   Investor

Contact info (address, e-mail, phone number):

_____

_____

_____

Name: _____

Relationship (circle one): Client   Friend   Adviser   Partner   Investor

Contact info (address, e-mail, phone number):

_____

_____

_____

Name: _____

Relationship (circle one): Client   Friend   Adviser   Partner   Investor

Contact info (address, e-mail, phone number):

_____

_____

_____

Name: _____

Relationship (circle one): Client   Friend   Adviser   Partner   Investor

Contact info (address, e-mail, phone number):

_____

_____

_____

PART 6

Glossary

GLOSSARY

Accounting—Keeping track of the money that goes in and out of the business.

Adaptability—Being flexible enough to change your plan when the original plan isn't working.

Advertising—Ways to tell people about your business. For example, flyers, TV commercials, radio messages, ads in the newspaper.

Assets—Things that your business owns, like supplies or equipment.

Balance—The total amount of money you have in a bank account.

Balance sheet—A form where you list your assets, liabilities, and net worth.

Bank—A place where you can keep your money safely. Banks can loan you money, give you checks, etc.

Budget—A plan for how to spend your money.

Capital—Money you use to start or run a business.

Certificate of deposit (CD)—This is a kind of bank account in which you give the bank a sum of money and agree to keep it in there for a certain amount of time. The bank issues you a certificate when you give them money, and after a certain amount of time you get your money back with interest.

Checking account—An account at the bank where you put your money. You can write checks instead of using cash to pay employees or buy things.

Client—A customer of your business.

Commission—A percentage of money that's paid when you sell something.

Contact—A client or other person who can be helpful to your business.

Customer—The person who buys your product or service.

Credit—When you don't have enough money to buy something, you can buy it on credit and pay for it later.

Debit—When you make a payment on something, the amount of money that comes out of your account is called a debit.

Debt—Money you owe to someone else, for example, a bank or an investor.

Deposit—To put money into a bank account.

Employees—People who work for you.

Entrepreneur—A term used for someone who starts his or her own business.

Expenses—Money from your business that you spend to buy supplies, pay employees, etc.

Income—Money you earn from working.

Interest—When you borrow money, interest is the amount you have to pay back in addition to what you borrowed.

Inventory—Products that you are waiting to sell.

Investment—When you put your money in a company, a business, or a fund, hoping to get more money back in return.

Investor—Somebody who loans you money to help start your business. The investor expects to be paid back more money than he or she invested.

Liability or liabilities—A debt or debts that you owe.

Loan—When a person gives you money that you have to pay back.

Loss—When you spend more money than you make.

Money market account—A bank account that requires you to keep a certain amount of money in the bank at all times. Money market accounts pay interest: more interest than a savings account but less interest than a certificate of deposit.

Mutual fund—An investment in which your money is used to purchase stock in many different companies. This decreases the risk of losing money.

Negotiation—The act of bargaining with someone until you can both agree on a deal.

Net worth—Your assets minus any liabilities you owe—it's what your business is worth.

Overhead—The ongoing cost of running your business.

Partner—A person with whom you start a business.

Percentage—A portion of money: for example, 10 percent of $100 is $10.

Product—An item you sell to customers.

Profit—The money you make from your business once you pay off the cost of running the business.

Real estate—Another name for property or land. That land may have houses, condominiums, or other structures on it.

Rent—What you pay to use space in a building for an office, shop, or factory.

Savings account—An account with a bank where you can keep your money to earn interest.

Services—Something you do for a customer in return for payment.

Start-up costs—Things you have to spend money on to get your business started. Some examples are flyers, posters, tools, and cleaning supplies.

Stocks—A piece of a company that you own.

Strategy—The master plan for your business.

Taxes—Money you owe the government. Income taxes are on income, and sales taxes are on sales of products.

Venture—A new business.

Withdraw—To take money out of a bank account.

Conclusion

Thank you for taking the time to read *Beyond the Lemonade Stand*. I hope you enjoyed it as much as I enjoyed writing it! I also hope it inspired you to think about the kind of moneymaking adventures *you'd* like to go on.

But even more than that, I hope you learned a thing or two about business and life. In the future, try to tackle both with energy and enthusiasm. If you do that, I know you can be a success!

Finally, after reading my book, I hope that you strike it rich—not just in money, but in happiness and love from your friends and your family.

If you have all of that, you really have made it big!

Sincerely,

Bill

Acknowledgments

There are so many people we would like to thank from the bottom of our hearts. Our mom, who spent many hours sharing her knowledge and writing talent with us. And our dad, who is looking down on us and smiling. Thank you to Mike Soenen and the three little angels Zack, Luke, and Noah, who loved listening to these stories and even contributed their own. Thanks to our sisters Beth and Katie and their families, who always support us. A special thank-you to Roger and Maureen Murray, who are the most creative people we know and have contributed their time and insights while making us laugh. A heartfelt thanks goes to our friends: many of them have been with us since the first grade, and others we picked up along the way but love and cherish just as much. John Plummer and Adam Andrezejewski, thanks for hangin' in there with us. And thanks to Jerry Agema, my first business partner as a kid, and Stuart Miller, who introduced me to the real estate business.

We would like to give a sincere thank-you to Mr. Trump, who started off the show with a lemonade stand and continues to "re-hire" me. Also to Greg Cuneo, who has taken me under his wing these past two years. To our right-hand people, Tommy Holl and Joanna Golebiowski, you have made our lives run smoothly through all of your hard work, and we appreciate that.

To our brilliant and talented editor, Kristen Pettit, whose knowledge, patience, and belief in us made this book possible, and to our publisher, Eloise Flood, who believed in us, thank you. Thanks to Amy DuVall, a gifted teacher of gifted students, and to her students at Pleasantdale Elementary School, who stayed in during recess to share their stories with us. To our agents, Jay Mandel and Jennifer Rudolph Walsh, thank you for all your guidance.